ISBN 978-1-5280-2249-1
PIBN 10901770

English
Français
Deutsche
Italiano
Español
Português

www.forgottenbooks.com

Mythology Photography **Fiction**
Fishing Christianity **Art** Cooking
Essays Buddhism Freemasonry
Medicine **Biology** Music **Ancient**
Egypt Evolution Carpentry Physics
Dance Geology **Mathematics** Fitness
Shakespeare **Folklore** Yoga Marketing
Confidence Immortality Biographies
Poetry **Psychology** Witchcraft
Electronics Chemistry History **Law**
Accounting **Philosophy** Anthropology
Alchemy Drama Quantum Mechanics
Atheism Sexual Health **Ancient History**
Entrepreneurship Languages Sport
Paleontology Needlework Islam
Metaphysics Investment Archaeology
Parenting Statistics Criminology
Motivational

CATALOGUE AND
PRICE LIST

1895

Small Fruit Plants

OF

FAIR VIEW FRUIT FARM

MOLINE, ILL.

plan
put
ing t
bougl
with
mi
pack

STONE, ORIGINATOR OF

Plow City, Stone's Early,

Gertrude and Governor

Fifer Strawberries

YELLOW SPICE RASPBERRY AND STONE'S
EARLY BLACKBERRY.

Announcement.

To my Friends and Patrons and all Lovers of Fine Fruit:

I desire to thank my old customers for the patronage extended to me in the past, and assure you that I shall endeavor to merit a continuance of favors in the future.

I hope to gain many new customers during the coming season, and solicit a trial order from those who have had no dealings w˙ with the assurance of giving satisfacti

All communications will receive and careful attention.   Respectfully,

CHARLES C. STONE,

Fairview Fruit Farm,

MOLINE, ILL.

TO OUR CUSTOMERS.

No Cheap Plants.

Read this catalogue carefully before ordering. No order booked for less than 75 cents. Stamps taken for sums less than $1. Will sell 6 of one variety at dozen rates, 50 at 100 rates and 500 at 1,000 rates. Parties wanting large orders write for special prices. Do not send to me for cheap plants, I do not grow them, I do not handle them, I do not plant them.

At Reduced Rates.

Estimates will be cheerfully furnished on plant orders. In many cases quotations may put it at less than catalogue rates, where stock ing surplus.

Shipped in Good Order.

my plants are well grown, true to name, are packed in the best possible manner, and are warranted to reach customers in good condition for planting, as fresh as if taken from their own ground. Anyone having cause for complaint will please state it promptly, and all mistakes will be corrected.

You Get What You Order.

In ordering write your name and address plainly, and you will receive an acknowledgment of the receipt of your order, and goods will be shipped as soon as season-opens. There will be no substitution of varieties, as you can rely upon getting what you order and nothing else. Many varieties have a local value, and selections for the family garden should be made from the best varieties that will do well over a wide range.

Mail or Express.

Add 20 cents per hundred on strawberries. If it be sent by mail, dozen rates, free. Please state in order whether to be sent by mail or express. Prices on larger quantities furnished on application. Buyer to pay express charges or freight.

Terms Strictly Cash.

Money may be sent at my risk by regis' letter, post office money order or ex money order, payable at Moline, Ill. Th press companies at Moline are the Adam the United States; the railroads, Chi. Rock Island & Pacific, Chicago, Burlington Quincy and Chicago, Milwaukee & St. Paul. I can pack and ship at short notice. My place is situated one and one-half miles from the express and postoffices.

Raspberry Plants

Sent only at dozen rates, prepaid. One hundred or 1,000 rates, sent by express or freight. purchaser paying charges. No charges for packing or crates. In packing strawberry plants for mailing I use the best quality of moss and waxed paper, that they may reach customers in the United States and Canada in good condition. In packing orders for express or freight, slat or ventilated crates will be used, with foliage, and tied in bunches of 25 or 50, as desired by purchaser. Raspberries packed so that the new shoots can not be broken off. In ordering raspberries get them out as early as the season and ground will permit.

Growing Raspberries.

In setting out raspberry plants, plow the land from 6 to 7 inches deep, harrow well, then harrow a little more later on, if the ground is not too wet to become soggy. Mark off your rows 7½ to 8 feet apart for black sorts. Set plants 3 to 3½ feet apart in the row. Do not put plants in a little hole with roots pointing to the moon, and then blame the man you bought your plants from. Try a potato fork with a boy hitched to it. Let the boy dig and mix the soil at the places where you need your plants, every 3 or 3½ feet, using a vessel or wooden bucket partly filled with water. Do not take over 25 plants at a time. With the aid of a plant trowel and your hands you can make a place for the plants to spread out roots in every direction. Plant from 4 to 5 inches deep, with the crown of the plant slightly covered, being careful not to break off the new shoots in packing soil on roots. A man and a boy can set 1,000 plants per day in this way, after the ground is prepared, with the loss of very few plants. Red sorts can be set the same way with rows from 6 to 8 feet apart, except Shafers.

REFERENCES.

C. F. HEMENWAY, Cashier First National Bank, Moline.

J. S. GILLMORE, Cashier Moline National Bank.

GEORGE STEVENS, Moline Plow Company.

J. SWANSON & Co., grocers. Moline.

HOLMGREN, ANDERSON & Co., grocers, Moline.

DR. J. W. STEWART, Moline.

BEDER WOOD, Moline.

The Plow City Strawberry.

BY CHARLES C. STONE.

In the year 1884 I sowed seed of Sharples and Atlantic, and quite a number of seedlings was the result. In 1886 my attention was called to a cluster of plants among the rest quite late in the season, by the large amount of fruit, the large size and fine color. I at once made preparation to give them a fair chance. By cultivating the plants that bore the fruit, five in number was the result in the spring of 1887. I had by selection thirty-eight plants, extra strong enes, and at least as many more that I left in the bed. In setting out the plants they all did well in three different locations and in different soil. Some of the plants set out in 1887 bore a full crop of fine berries the past hot and dry season of 1894, and can be seen standing for 1895 healthy and vigorous, having a stool of twelve to fourteen inches across. The plants are large and robust, and of a bright green color, and have never, in the eight years, showed any sign of blight, rust or defect of any kind, and have never failed to bear an enormous crop of the finest and largest berries raised on my place. The Plow City is in bearing late to very late, the season extending from June 15 to July 25. It has a strong and perfect blossom with heavy, light green foliage, and strong tall fruit stalks. It is from ten to fifteen inches long, with ten to twenty large berries on each of the four to seven fruit stalks to each plant when two years old. I have often counted from 80 to 100 berries on one year old plants. In the year 1893, from four rows sixty-six feet long, 211 quarts of Plow City Strawberries were picked by one picker and sold, besides a great many that were carried away for samples. Eight boxes were sent to the World's Fair, each box containing respectively, 12, 13, 13, 14, 14, 15, 16 and 17 berries in Hallock quart boxes. One plant sent at the same time, one year old, had 192 perfect berries and blossoms.

□ For reference would mention W. C. Wilson or J. W. Warr, editor of *The Western Plowman*, who have picked sample berries that measured eleven and one-half inches in circumference.

I will say of the 227 varieties that have fruited with me, and many thousand seedlings in the past eighteen years, the Plow City simply leads them all.

Please note the testimony of different growers on the same subject, also that of Prof. E. S. Goff, Wisconsin Experiment Station, Madison, Wis.; Mr. John Little, of Granton, Ont., or Mr. Bedar Wood, of Moline, who have had a large experience in raising fine seedlings. The "Proof of the pudding is in the eating." Therefore do not get left, but buy a dozen plants.

The following description of the Plow City strawberry is from Mr. W. C. Wilson of South Moline, a grower of small fruits, with an experience of thirty years, who is well qualified to speak regarding the merits of the Plow City Strawberry :

In the endeavor to describe the new strawberry originated by C. C. Stone, of this place, the statements necessary to tell the actual truth regarding it must seem to the practical fruit grower almost preposterous. Before saying anything of the berry I desire to say that I have grown all the leading berries from the days of the Hovey, Wilson, Albany, Jocunda, etc. I have, to my sorrow, also, tested most of the highly advertised fakes of the Eastern nurseries. I have been called a successful strawberry grower and have had some immense crops, but until I visited Mr. Stone's place and saw the Plow City in fruit, I never fully realized the possibilities of strawberry culture. In 1893 I visited Mr. Stone's place some four times, at intervals of three or four days, and under conditions far from being the most favorable, and found the Plow City eclipsing everything I ever saw in the way of strawberries Its special points of merits were :

First — Size.

Second — Symmetry, being even in size, with few rough berries.

Third — Color, being of an even, uniform color, with no green tips or hard cores.

Fourth —Flavor, being much better than the average berry.

Fifth —Firmness, would rank it with the Jersey in this locality.

Sixth —Season, being one of the latest, or, rather, having one of the longest seasons of any berry I ever saw. Mr. Stone, for several years has had these berries, fine large ones at that, in the market long after all other growers were out of the market.

Seventh —Yield. My standard of comparison is the Warfield, Crescent or the Lovett, and I actually believe that the Plow City in 1893 would have doubled the yield of any of them at their best.

In 1894 I visited the Plow City but once, and in one of the most unfavorable seasons I ever experienced, and under most adverse conditions found it giving a good account of itself. In that year no berries were ripened properly, especially the larger varieties. Lovett or Warfield, I think, excelled the Plow City in color during the past year, but it was quite up to the Jersey, Bubach, Gaudy or Parker early on this point during the past year. Mr. Stone's fruiting patch was on an exposed, dry ridge, not half mulched, and suffered severely by late frosts and the drouth, so that 1894 was really no test. I believe that most of my brother growers in this vicinity will concede that I had the best crop grown near here in 1894. This was largely due to an unusually heavy mulch and protection from our May frosts. My berries were also among the latest, yet Mr. Stone was marketing the Plow City, in quantity, more than a week after my last Gaudy was gone.

Among several hundred seedlings that Mr. Stone has grown and tested is another of rare value, a berry named the Gertrude, that is going to take the place of all others of its season in this neighborhood as soon as we can get the plants.

I, at least, expect to plant all I can afford to buy of each of these berries as soon as they are on the market.

Should Mr. Stone see fit to use this description of his berries as I see them, I trust no one will write to me for plants, as I have none, nor no interest whatever in them.

W. C. WILSON.

We visited Mr. Stone's place during the years named, and endorse every statement made by Mr. Wilson.

H. E. BIGGS, Proprietor Prospect Park Restaurant.

M. J. McENIRY, Postmaster, Moline, Ill.

J. W. WARR, Editor *Western Plowman*.

BEDER WOOD.

FRANK B. SUMAN, Police Station.

CHARLES HENDERSON, Fruit Grower.

VICTOR HENDERSON, Fruit Grower.

The Gertrude Strawberry.

BY CHARLES C. STONE.

The Gertrude strawberry was a chance seedling found growing among some grape vines on my place in 1887 by my daughter Gertrude, from whom it derives its name. It has been carefully tested on different soils, has large, tall, bright green foliage that protects its blossoms from frost. Among known varieties, this is one of the earliest to mature. It ripens with the Beder Wood, Sadie Mitchell, and other early sorts, being larger than any early variety, and ranking in size with Sharpless, Bubach, Gaudy. It holds well to the last picking, resembles the Edgar Queen in shape and has no ill-shaped berries. It is of a pleasing, bright scarlet color, very attractive, the coloring being even with no white tips. Its flesh is firm and of good quality. The plant is a marvel of beauty and is a treat to look at. It has no sign of rust or other defect about it and is exceedingly productive. During the past season it bore a profitable crop of fruit, notwithstanding the discouraging conditions of the extreme drouth that prevailed from the time fruit was set out up to nearly five weeks, and this, too, with ordinary field culture.

The blossoms are large and perfect, and well supplied with the much desired pollen, making it a grand pollenizer for other large pistillate sorts, namely, the Bubach, Edgar Queen, Greenville, Timbrell and Haverland, which in foliage closely resembles the latter.

CHARLES C. STONE.

AGREEMENT.

I hereby agree not to sell, trade, or in any way dispose of plants of the Plow City Strawberry at less than the originator's price for the fall of 1895 or spring of 1896, said prices to be as follows: Per 12, $2.50; per 25, $5.00; per 50, $10.00; per 100, $20.00; per 1,000 $150.00.

Prices for spring and fall of 1895: Per 12, $5.00; per 25, $10.00; per 50, $20.00. Not more than fifty plants sold to any one person for spring of 1895.

Price List

OF

Strawberry Plants

	Per 12	Per 100	Per 1,000
Plow City	$5 00	......	......
Gertrude	2 00	$10 00	......
[HS] Splendid	1 00	3 00	$20 00
[HS] Cyclone	1 00	......	......
[P] Aroma	1 00	......	......
[P] Eureka	50	1 50	......
[S] Governor Fifer	1 00	6 00	......
[S] Hartsell	1 00	6 00	......
[S] Henry Ward Beecher	1 50	......	......
[S] Childs	75	4 00	......
[S] Leader	75	1 50	.. .
[S] Lovets	50	1 50	......
[P] Haverland	50	1 75	4 00
[P] Great Pacific	50	1 00	......
[S] Edward Favorite	75	2 00	......
[S] Enhance	75	1 50	......
E. Proe, worthless	....	......	......
Westbrook, no good	....	......	......
[P] Jay Gould	75	1 50	......
[P] Bissel	75	3 00	12 00
[S] Belle	1 00	4 00	......
[S] Alton	75	3 00	......
[P] Bubach	50	1 50	......
[S] Beder Wood	50	1 00	4 00
[S] Sherman	1 00	2 00	......
[S] Dayton	75	2 00	......
[S] Muskingum	75	2 00	......
[S] Beverly	75	2 00	......

[P]	Ed. Gunn	75	1 00	. . . . . .
[S]	Rio 1 00		4 00	. . . . . .
[S]	Mrs. Cleveland	75	2 00	. . . . . .
[P]	Greenville	75	1 50	. . . . . .
[S]	Phillips	75	2 00	. . . . . .
[S]	Iocunda, improved . .	75	. . . . . .	. . . .
[S]	Thomson's 40	50	1 50	. . . . . .
[P]	Thomson's 31	50	1 50	. . . . . .
[P]	Sadie	50	1 25	. . . . . .
[S]	Middlefield	75	1 75	. . . . . .
[S]	Sandoval	50	1 00	. . . . . .
[S]	Governor Hoard . . .	50	1 00	. . . . . .
[S]	Captain Jack	50	80	. . . . . .
[P]	Princess	50	1 25	. . . . . .
[P]	Berton's Eclipse . . .	50	1 00	. . . . . .
[P]	C'escent Trip	50	75	. . . . . .
[S]	Mrs. Cleveland	75	2 00	. . . . . .
[S]	Mystic 1 00		5 00	. . . . . .
[S]	Northern	75	2 00	. . . . . .
[S]	Ohio Centennial . . . 1 00		. . . . . .	. . . . . .
[S]	Parker Earl	75	1 50	. . . . . .
[S]	Pearl	75	2 00	. . . . . .
[P]	P. Chief 1 00		4 00	. . . . . .
[P]	Princess Sudd	75	1 25	. . . . . .
[P]	Regina	50	1 00	. . . . . .
[S]	Robison	75	2 00	. . . . . .
[S]	Saunders	75	1 50	. . . . . .

Prize, Watson, Maple, Bank, Cruses No. 9, Hull's Nos. 1, 6 and 8, Effie May and Hope — these nine under restrictions.

Some sixty others of newer introductions and seedlings of my own on trial of great merit.

$2.50 Collection.

[12P] Sadie, strawbery, early and productive $0 40
[12S] Gaudy, strawberry, late plants . . 50
[12S] Edgar Queen, strawberry 50
[12S] Beder Wood, strawberry 50

[2S] Gertrude, strawberry plants   40
[6] Palmer, raspberry plants   25
[6] Older seedling raspberry plants . . .   25
[12] Gregg, best late raspberry plants . .   40

By express . . . . $ 3 20

$7.00 Collection.

[3S] Plow City, strawberry, new plants,
  best grade $0 80
[6S] Gertrude, best new large early raspberry 1 00
[12S] Governor Fifer, medium new strawberry 1 00
[12P] Princess, strawberry   50
[12S] Beauty, strawberry, large and fine .   75
[12S] Sherman, strawberry   75
[12] Palmer, raspberry, best early black .   50
[12] Kansas, raspberry, large and fine . .   75
[12] Older, raspberry, best medium . . .   75
[1] Yellow Spice. raspberry, new yellow .   50
[12] Shafer's Colossal, raspberry   50

                                      $ 7 80

$6.20 Collection for $5.00.

[1S] Plow City, best late strawberry . . .$0 40
[3S] Gertrude, best large early strawberry   50
[6S] Governor Fifer, medium to late new   50
[6S] Beauty, new fine large   40
[12P] Haverland, very productive   35
[12S] Beverly, large fine medium   50
[12S] Parker's Earl, one of the best late .   50
[12P] Sadie, early and productive   50
[12] Palmer, early black raspberry   50
[12] Older. best large black medium raspberry   75
[12] Gregg, best large late black   50
[12] Turner, red hardy productive   40
[12] Shaffer's Colossal, best large purple .   50

                                      $ 6 20

$10.00 Collection of Strawberry and Raspberry Plants.

[6] Gertrude, best large new early . . . . $ 1 00
[25] Beder Wood, early strawberry . . . 1 00
[3] Plow City, best new large late 1 20
[25] Gaudy, strawberry, late 1 00
[12] Governor Fifer, strawberry, medium 1 00
[25] Haverland. strawberry, medium . . 60
[25] Parker Earl, strawberry 1 00
[25] Palmer, raspberry, first early 75
[25] Gregg, best large late 50
[25] Older, best large medium 1 00
[25] Kansas, new large early 1 00
[12] Shafer's Colossal, large purple . . . 50
[6] Muskingum, raspberry, new purple . 25
[2] Yellow Spice, raspberry. new yellow . 1 00
[1] Plant, new advance raspberry, early
black 1 00
                                        _____
                                        $12 80
This collection by express 10 00

Raspberries

Palmer.

Best of all early raspberries ; have tested it for three years ; is far ahead of Souhegan or Tyler. It is hardy, early, large size, good in quality and productive fruit, jet black. Dozen, 75 cents ; hundred, $1.50 ; thousand, $10.00.

Kansas.

Next to Palmer in earliness, larger than Gregg, more productive and hardier and a good shipper. Orders shculd be sent in early to secure good plants, as all will be called for. Dozen, 75 cents ; hundred, $2.50 : thousand. $18.00.

Older.

Ripens after Kansas, is as large as Grcgg, with small seeds, jet black, with thick juice, hangs on the bushes well and stands drouth well. Dozen, 75 cents : hundred, $1.50 : thousand, $13.00.

Gregg.

This is the stand-by for a late variety, it is one of the latest black caps. Dozen, 75 cents : hundred, $1.25 ; thousand, $9.00.

Souhegan or Tyler.

Too well-known to need any description.

Dozen, 75 cents; hundred, $1.25; thousand $8.00.

Shafers.

The largest red raspberry grown, larger than Gregg, purple in color. Dozen, 75 cents; hundred, $1.50; thousand, $11.00.

Muskingum.

A new variety coming from Ohio. It resembles Shafers very close, the plants being more compact in growth and fully as polific, if not more so. The flesh is also hardier. Dozen. 75 cents.

Brandywine.

A red raspberry, late, and a good shipper. Dozen, 75 cents; hundred, $1.00; thousand, $8.00.

Turner.

One of the oldest raspberries, but a stand-by here. Dozen, 75 cents; hundred, $1.00; thousand, $8.00.

Blackberries

Snyder.

This variety is old and well-known. It will stand the severest cold without injury and is of excellent quality. Dozen, 50 cents; hundred, $1.00; thousand, $9.00.

Stone's Hardy.

This superior blackberry originated in Wisconsin, and can be relied upon as being the hardiest; also sweet and productive, weighing its strong canes to the ground with fruit, and larger than Snyder. Dozen, 50 cents; hundred, $1.50; thousand, $10.00.

Taylor Prolific.

A good companion for Snyder, a variety of great hardiness and productive, ripens some-what later, berries much larger and of fine flavor. Its merits are not well-known. Dozen, 50 cents; hundred, $1.50; thousand, $10.00.

Stone's Early.

A chance seedling found growing on my place in 1888; short, stocky bush, very hardy fruit, nearly round, flavor excellent, foilage thick, and fruit heavy, about the size of Snyder, ripens ten days earlier, always matures its entire crop, never fails, enormously productive, one of the best. Price, 50 cents each; $5.00 per dozen.

In sending raspberry plants we can send by freight if ordered early, otherwise will send by express. Rates by mail free, purchaser paying freight and express charges. Packing and crates free. Put on car or at express office.

TESTIMONIALS.

These are a few of the many words of praise from growers of different states on receiving plants from me :

CLEVELAND NURSERY CO., RIO VISTA, VA.— We received your plants to-day, all O K.

ED HULL, OLYPHANT, PA.—I received a package of strawberry plants from you to-day. In fine condition they were, not even wilted.

AMERICAN FARM AND HORTICULUURIST, RIO VISTA. VA.—Your Stone's Early or No. 1 have done well this year.

FRANK A. DRUHL, SCOTT COUNTY, IOWA—I have seen the Plow City strawberry growing on Mr. Stone's farm and would say it is the best, largest and finest I have ever seen. It is the most productive, has fine, healthy foliage and the very best of flavor.

HOLMGREN, ANDERSON & CO., MOLINE, ILL.— In giving our testimony of the Plow City strawberry; would say that we could never get enough of them. They are really the largest berry we have ever sold, and the flavor is perfect.

B. J. MESSER, DAVENPORT, IOWA—In regard to your new strawberries that I saw growing in your field last summer, I would say that the Gertrude is an early berry, extraordinary in size, productiveness, beauty and quality, having a strong plant. The Plow City is a late berry, a very strong grower and produces heavy crops of fine, large fruit.

MRS. L. N. WARNER, WATERTOWN, ILL.—1 can say for the Plow City as a late berry, it has a fine appearance on your grounds, a luxuriant growth and very productive color. The berries are large and firm and of good flavor and seem to be a very promising variety.

C. HENDERSON, SOUTH MOLINE, ILL.—We are well acquainted with Mr. Stone as an honorable fruit grower and an earnest horticulturist. and he has something growing on his place in strawberries. He keeps to the front in all leading sorts. but Gertrude, as an early, large, productive berry, Plow City as a late, large and most productive berry, we have never seen their equal.

F. L. ROSSER, BRITTAIN, O.—Your plants in good condition. I think every one will grow.

VICTOR HENDERSON, MOLINE, ILL.—I have carefully watched the small fruit farm of C. C. Stone, as he is a neighbor fruit grower. As he is an earnest horticulturist he succeeds in producing more good novelties than any other man of his age. In two varieties they surpass any thing of the kind that I have ever seen. If I was confined to two varieties they would be the Gertrude for early and the Plow City for late.

B. J. MESSER SCOTT COUNTY, IOWA—We set the strawberry plants received from you Friday. Fine, large plants they are. All doing well, but we need some rain.

J. M. HOLT, MOLINE, ILL.—This is to certify that I have used the Plow City strawberry grown by C. C. Stone, of the Fairview fruit farm at South Moline, Ill., and found it one of the best flavored and best canning berries that I have ever used.

JOHN PIERCE, SOUTH MOLINE, ILL.—I have watched Mr. Stone's new seedlings for several years, as he has the largest collection that I know of, from the earlies to the extreme late, Stone's Early Gertrude being fine early sort, Plow City being very late, and combining more good points than any berries I have ever seen.

CASSELL NURSERY CO., COVINGTON, O.—Beder Wood plants received in fine shape.

D. L. BISSELL, TENTI, ILL.—The plants came to hand in fine shape. Very nice plants.

C. F. TREFT, SCOTT COUNTY, IOWA—Strawberry plants looking nicely, but need rain.

P. SUTTON, EXETER, PA.—Your plants received after being delayed 19 days. but not your fault. Plants look quite fresh for the time and most of them will grow, I think.

S. H. WARREN, WESTON, MASS.—Your plants are received in good shape. Thanks

E. S. GOFF, MADISON, WIS.—In reply to yours of the 11th ult., I have delayed my reply until the strawberry season is nearly over in order that I might give a more intelligent report. The plants came late in the spring of 1892 and did not make a very good growth. They have borne well and the fruit is of large size and good quality. The fruit holds its size very well indeed. Next season I shall have an opportunity to give a better idea of its productiveness. I consider it one of our promising sorts.

BENJ. M. SMITH, BEVERLY, MASS,—Strawberry plants came this evening in splendid condition, finely packed.

DAVID KELSO, SOUTH MOLINE, ILL.—Upon my ground in field and test bed I have about 200 varieties, comprising nearly all the standard varieties known to the public, and many new sorts. On trial, from careful observation during several seasons past, I regard, all points considered, the following two varieties to be the best of their season yet introduced: Gertrude for early and Plow City for late.

BEDER WOOD — For productiveness, size, color, flavor and firmness, I consider your Plow City very fine as I saw it on your ground.

E. S GOFF, UNIVERSITY OF WISCONSIN EXPERIMENT STATION. MADISON, WIS.—The Plow City is one of our promising new strawberries.

E. J. SCOFIELD, HANOVER, WIS.—Plow City, as seen in fruiting on the originator's grounds at Moline, Ill., June, '94, was certainly making a very fine show of fruit. Berries large, late and plenty of them; plants robust and apparently healthy, although they were suffering for want of rain, as the ground in the bed was cracked open in many places a quarter of an inch. If it will do as well in general as it does on the grounds of the originator it will prove a success.

CPSIA information can be obtained
at www.ICGtesting.com
Printed in the USA
BVHW061644031218
534640BV00036B/3260/P

9 781528 022491